KW-483-050

INTERNET

WORLD OF TEENAGERS

Written By

SAGAR CHANDOLA

Copyright by Sagar Chandola in 2014

INTERNET

WORLD OF TEENAGERS

"I dedicate this book to my all family members and relatives for their support"

SAGAR CHANDOLA

Special Thanks

I would like to thank my teachers and authorities of my collage **Chhotu Ram Rural Institute of Technology (crrit)** for promoting me as a speaker or consultant. This book would never be completed if my teachers didn't support me for this. This collage gave a big platform to me for starting my carrier. This is my second book and without the consulting of my teachers of **crrit** I couldn't be write this. So I would like to thanks all my teachers, principals who gave courage to me for this book and promote me as a speaker or author.

Preface

This book is totally based on social life of teenagers which they spend on the internet. In which you will get a lot of advantages or disadvantages of internet while using by teenagers in their own way which they actually don't know. They don't know that what can be happen on internet if they use it any wrong way because today every teenager wants to become cool, stylish, etc. for which he takes the help of internet but sometimes they do some mistakes on it which can become a very big problem for them. So, if you also a teenager and spend your most of time on internet you should be read this book because you don't know that you are playing a serious game with your life while using internet which can destroy you if you don't understand it and for this there are so many ways which has explained in this book with a very sensitive language. All the topics of this book are very important for every teenager who is using internet a lot of. You will get some tips in this book which can help you to prevent yourself from the wars of internet and remember that you have to be serious while reading this book because it is not a joke "you are playing with your life while using internet" So be careful because your one mistake can destroy you on the internet and your whole life will become like a shadow which means there is no any hope without black.

About Author

Sagar Chandola is a 17 years old ethical hacker, speaker, author, web developer and designer from India and pursuing diploma in Digital Electronics from Chhotu Ram Rural Institute Of Technology. He is motivational speakers who provides seminars and workshops on ethical hacking or cyber security and introduce them from it. His first book "A Tour Of Ethical Hacking" was big hit in which he introduced the ethical hacking from basic to advance and written for specially those beginners who want to start their carrier in cyber security.

Aim of this book

This book has been written only for those teenagers who are using the internet for making fun and spend their whole day on it because they think that it just a way to make fun but the truth behind of it is totally different. There are so many dangers on the internet which always attract the teenagers and most of teenagers has been attacked and make their life very cheap. This book is only a medium to tell the teenagers about the advantages, disadvantages of internet because on internet a small mistake can become a very big trouble for you and the effect of that mistake will be very dangerous. So, if you are a teenager who loves the internet and spend your time a lot of on internet then you should be read this book which can be very helpful to you. By this book you can understand the truth of internet which hide into it and never see when we use a lot of. So, remember always while using internet that your one mistake on internet can become a very big problem for you.

--- SAGAR CHANDOLA

CONTENTS

"Best of luck to all of you teen-agers who are reading this book and I hope that you will understand that what I would like to say actually"

SAGAR CHANDOLA

Introduction to Internet

In this topic we first we read about the Internet basics in which we will study that "What is the Internet","Uses of Internet","Ways to use Internet" because it is more important to know for all of us. I know that this topic will boared you but there is no any way to start direct so I started from the basics. It will be theortically but don't worry because this topic is not very long and all the sections of this topic has been explained by me in a very short way but all the topics are neccessory to know so do not leave any topic and now we start to read about Internet. Which is a global network actually and connects a billion of devices worldwide on the base of TCP/IP. We can find anything on Internet very easily because of its world wide connected system. We know it as **WWW** which means **World Wide Web** because it is just like a web which connects everyone to each other from one end to another end of the world. The main matter is that to know "how the internet works actually" because this is the very basic thing which you must be have to know if you are in the IT field or want to go into it. There are so many things on which the internet or www works in which protocols, servers, dns, etc contains.

So, basically Internet works step by step everytime and without performing the step according to their setup it can't be work so you can be understand that how the all things are necessory to perform according their steps or works. Have you think ever that how you get the results o internet when you type something on it? Whenever you type something on web then first it checks that query and if it is possible or in the database then it gives the access to you otherwise you get the error message which you have seen many times whenever you not get connect to the internet.

Uses of Internet : As we know that what is the importance of Internet in our today's life because now we are totally depending upon it. Internet becomes a necessary requirement for everyone now whereas we use it for our any work or making fun. Because of Internet our daily life become so easy like if we want to send any letter then we simply send it thorugh email by using any online email service on internet and the best thing is that mail will send into just 2-10 seconds only. Another example of internet is that if we want to shopping then we can easily buy anything from Internet by using any ecommerce website. There are so many uses of Internet like these which has been given below:

- ✓ We can pay any type of bill very easily by using internet whereas we are in any part of the world.
- ✓ By using Internet we can find any type of information in just a few minutes.
- ✓ We can study any topic on internet very easily without taking any special coaching.
- ✓ If we want to communicate with someone if we are in any part of the world then we can easily talk to him by using internet.

Sot,these are some examples which we can easily do with the help of Internet in few minutes and because of it our busy life becomes easy. The best part of the internet is that we don't need any special coaching to learn it so anybody can use it easily. These are the some uses and advantages of Internet which we can do very easily and now we read our next topic in which we will know that what are the ways to use Internet because we need to know first about it that how we can access the internet, what requirements we need to access it.

Ways to use Internet : Today Internet is everywhere as you see and the requirements are also increasing day be day for it. A lot of devices has come on which we can access the internet from anywhere or any part of the world. The most ways which we use generally for Internet are only the mobile phones and computers because they are just like a craze whenever we gonna into them then it is very difficult for everyone to leave out from here. With increasing of Internet services the technology is also increasing in a very fast way because first the Internet is more expensive and we need a special device if we want to access it but now it is like a craze because we can see the use of Internet everywhere as you know that. Today a lot of technical specifications has been come like wifi, broadband, etc by which we can easily use the Internet anywhere on our computers, laptops, mobile phones. I think that wifi is the best way to use Internet because we do not need any cable or modem for it simply connect the device with router and access the Internet. Here are the techniques or technical specifications ways by which we use the Internet.

Modem

It is the main part which we need if we want to access Internet because receives and transfers the signals to web for connecting with it. If there is no modem device then we can not access the Internet.Their are two parts of modem generally which are internal modem and external modem and both have been explained below as you can see for your better understand.

➤ Internal Modem

It is the oldest method in which a modem is already includes into your computer so it is known as the internal modem and the main thing is that the size of this modem was very old and for setup it we need a very long process which was so mindfreaking so many of users were don't use it. Another problem with it that we need any dial up connection which can connect with it and for it we need any landline phone otherwise we can't use it.

➢ External Modem

It is the new and latest way which came after internal modems in which we need any other device or dial up connection. In external modem there is only a single device which is small in size and it is the modem also but the good thing is that we can use it anywhere and for this we don't need any special connection. Simply setup a external modem device and access the internet. The best wasy to understand the external modem is the broadband which we use today a lot of for access internet anywhere. Broadband is the best example of an external modem in which we simply plug a device which is actually a modem and after pugging it we can access the internet easily.

Dial up Connection

Broadband Connection or device

➢ WI-FI

I think that wifi is the best way to use internet for everyone because in wifi we don't need any special cable or setup. We only need a wifi router and a device on which we will access the internet and simply connect that device with router and access the internet. But the good thing is that we can easily connect a lot of devices with one router without using any cable and access the internet. There are so many types of wifi routers with their different specifications or works. Today most of offices, companies, communities, schools, etc are using wifi because of its good compatibility

These are the ways to use Internet which both are different from each together. Now you decide that which is good for you from both of these. As you know that Internet become a very neccessory requirement for everyone in today's life and the users of it are increasing day by day so I think that in future a lot of more facilites will develop which help to you in access of Internet more easily because the craze of Internet will never go from any mind who use it.

Internet for teenagers

Today we are living in a technical world where we totally depend upon the technology and our use of it is increasing day by day which make us more comfortable. There are so many facilities given by internet which we use everyday in our life in which the most imporatant topic is the "Internet" as I think because there is no any person as I think which don't know about the Internet. So you can suppose from this "how much the craze of Internet" in everyone's life. Today's generation is modern totally as you know. Yeah!! You are right friends I am talking about teeanagers which knows evertything about technology that "how to use it, how to explore it". You can take a real example from your life that how the youngsters use internet or technology you can see. But have u ever think that what is the magic which made the teenagers crazy for Internet because approx. 98% teenagers are using a lot Internet in their daily life which means that they have made it their life where they have no limit.

Internet become like a game for teenagers now because they use it for making fun only like sharing, uploading, downloading, playing, etc. The matter is only that how they are using it? Because most of teenagers use the internet for making fun not their work whereas internet is for help not to fun because if it can help you then also destroy you if you use it badly. Most of the teenagers think that on internet they can make their private world where they have no rules but the reality is totally different from it. Internet is a very helpful for teenagers because today they can study here, taking help in their projects, get their answers, etc but the reality is totally different from this because 80% teenagers do not use the internet in a right way. They use it for making fun only but they don't know that what they are doing actually. They don't want to understand the reality of internet which is behind on it. If you are a teenager also then first ask a question to yourself that "are you use the internet correctly or not?" because it's related with your life or your future. Today internet means only a medium to make fun for most of teenagers or youngsters specially those who are in collage or school because of competition only. The craze of internet is a very important topic for every teenager because if he got entered into the world of Internet then he can't take it outside. So, you need to understand it first or you have to know about the reality behind Internet before to use it otherwise you can be into a large trouble which can destroy your life very easily. You should be understand the Internet actually in which you have to know about its advantages and disadvantages.

➢ Craze of Internet

As you know that everything has two parts first is good another is bad and you should be know the both. If you are a youngster and using Internet or spend your whole day on it then you need to be alert now because you don't know that you are playing with a danger which can destroy you into few minutes also if you perform any mistake. You can ask from youngsters or see them that what is the value of Internet in their lifes by which you can be understand the craze of Internet which approx. every teenager or youngster have in today's world. Craze of Internet is a can become very dangerous for you and if you get into it then you can't be leave it. This topic is very important for all of youngsters because most of youngsters got webbed because of only the craze of Internet. The main problem of this generation is only that they don't want to understand anything and that's why they don't know about the reality behind of anything which they use. Same for the internet on which they spend their whole day and perform their activites. Internet is a free place for them where they have no privacy, no rules and that's why they do some activities on it which can become so dangrous and get them into trouble but they don't understand because of their craze of Internet. The age of 16-18 is the most important age for evry youngster because in this age they don't have smartness so anyone can divert their mind very easily. All the youngsters of this age have very creative mind which can divert on anything. So, in this age the duty of parents is only that to see their children activities which they perform. If they use Internet then the parents should be check them that what are they doing on it because if they got into the craze of Internet then it will be effect on their future and can destroy it very easily. Parents should be give a smart locality to their children which gives smartness to them.

Internet is not a bad thing if you use it correctly because it can help you in so many of your work which makes easy because of Internet. The only thing you should be remember while using it that do not get into the craze of it because if it is helpful another side it can become a very dangrous for you. Always remember that "Internet is like a weapon if you use it badly because it can destroy your whole life forever on you one wrong activity which you performed on it" so always be smart and think while using it.

Attraction of Internet

Attraction of anything is a very bad thing for everyone because if someone attracts towards anything and get into it then he can do anything without understanding the reality behind of that thing. But now we are talking about the Internet which always try to attract you whenever you see it now the choice is yours that you choose it or not because the attraction of Internet is very high and it will make you crazy if you get into it. Most of teenagers destroy their lifes on web when they got crazy for it a lot of. I tell you a truth about Internet that is whenever you are in collage then you become crazy for it because of your locality and you can easily understand it by taking your own life example that what u see between your friends group I think 80% friends talk about the Internet which means chatting, gossip, social media, etc and this is too much for you to attract towards Internet. You can undertand that what I would like to say or undertand that how you get attract towards Internet in your real life.

 Now take a real example from our life which we see generally in your locality and we see that 98% teenagers have a good smartphones, gadets, etc only for showoff because the thinking of teenagers now is only for their comparison. Nobody wants to become small between their locality. And for this situation the most helpful thing is for them only "Internet". Yeah I am right because as I think every teenager use Internet and learn a lot of things which are intresting for them and when he got crazed then he shares it with their friends. So, basically it just like a chain but the difference is only that some youngsters take it and some not. But atually those teenagers who don't get into it they become safe and those who crazed they got them into a danger which atually they don't know about it.

In the age of teenagers they can't decide that what they should be do because they have the creative mind which follow the others always. But sometimes it will become a danger for them because of their craze. The main topic is here that what they think when they do mistake on Internet because they don't know actually that any small mistake on Internet can effect on their whole life and they will not any chace to fix it again. I would like to suggest those teenagers who are using the Internet only for make fun that you need to be understand the reality of

Internet because you don't know that you are playing with danger actually and this is not only a one time danger if it attacks then you can lost your whole life here forever. This is important for every youngster to know the real world of Internet which hidden behind it because you use Internet as a fun whereas you don't guess that what can the resulf of this and I can only say that the result of it will be very bad for everyone who is using Internet as a fun.

I hope that you have been understood that what I would like to say. So these are some important topics about teenagers and Internet which can be a danger for everyone. So, always think that what are u doing while using Internet. Fun or crime? Because it is very important to know.

Why teenagers use Internet?

This topic is for those parents whose children use the Internet a lot of and spend their whole day on it because it is more important for every parent to know that what is the cause for which their children use the Internet a lot of and make their crazy for it. Internet is like a magical world where you can do anything which u want so that's why every teenager attract towards it because they have made it a medium to make fun a lot. In this topic you will get some main and important facts of Internet by which most of teenagers use it. While reading these all facts you should be remember that these all are those ways which you or your friends, children, etc are using only for making fun so now your duty is to tell them about it that how it can become a very big danger for them if they use it a lot of but only for making fun because on Internet there are so many people who can cheat you very easily if you don't follow the safety. You need to follow safety first while using Internet because it is very easy to cheat someone's on internet because here anybody can hide his privacy easily or he can also use privacy of someone which will be known for you but actually the truth is totally different from it because he is not that person which you known otherwise it is the criminal who cheats you. So, understand the realities of Internet which got hidden behind it because it just like a fake world. Now see the main topics which I have given below and very important for everyone to understand who are using them a lot because you don't know that what can be happen if you mistake ever on it.

➢ Social Media

Before start the topic first I would to ask a question to you that what you see common in most of teenagers while they use internet. I mean to say that what they do on Internet which makes them crazy for it. And I know that you will say "Chatting" and it is the truth. Because today 90% of teenagers got crazy for chatting or messanging and this makes esy for them because of social media websites where they can do it very esily. But not only chatting they can also get connect with others on social media by which they can make new friends online but what the cause behind it which makes them crazy for it have you think ever? It is very important to know because I think that 98% of youngsters are on social media today and spend their 80% of day on it.

Social media is not a bad for us but it depends on us that how we use it actually and that is the topic on which we have to think. Social media has become a part of life for every teenager and it become like a medium to make fun for them which they actually do. Now the question is for evryone that what is the reason behind social media which makes the teenagers crazy for it. And for it here are the some feature of social media has been given below which attracts the most of youngsters towards social media and they become crazy for it.

- ✓ Here they can make a lot of friends from any part of the world.
- ✓ They can play intresting games here.
- ✓ Chatting or messaging with someone else he is in any part of the world.
- ✓ Get connected with your society, friends, community.
- ✓ Uploading your photos which you can show others and become popular between them.

✓ **They can share anything with their friends which they want.**

So, these are some facts about social media which are intresting for everyone and that's why most of youngsters use it as you know. Social media is only like a medium to make fun for them where they can share, upload, do anything without rules. Today social media has become important for every teenager and every teen wants it.

So, this is the important of social media for a teenager which we read in previous topic in which we read that how teenagers use it but now we have need to know the reality of it that how the social media can affects on your life and how the dangerous it will be or it ca n be. As you know that everything has the two parts in which first is good another is bad only the choice is yours that what you choose. I am saying about social media which become a medium to make fun for every teenager today but they don't know that actually they are playing with danger and it will affect on their life which will be very hearted. The way which they are using to use social media is totally wrong as I think and it is only a danger for all of them which they can't see because of their craze to use social media. Now we take an example of the top social media website which is using be every teenager today and that is one an only "Facebook". You also know that how the facebook makes crazy everyone and attracts toward it. But what is going on facebook you know because everyone use it. But the question is for every teenager that how longer it is safe because today social media has become a best friend of every teenager where they upload their all activity which they don't need to share actually. Here are some activities given below which a teen perform on social media:

✓ Uploading of photos and share them with everyone
✓ Make unknown friends without any information
✓ Share their all information with everyone

- ✓ **Provide their contact information or details to everyone**
- ✓ **Chat with everyone who are strangers for them**

So, these are some activities which every teenager performs today on social media and use it only for these type of activities even facebook or other social media websites. These all like only a fun for them but the truth is totally different and when it comes then it only affects on the life of them. They don't know that what they are doing actually because they got crazy for it. But now it is most important for you to know the reality which has hidden behind it and can become very dangerous for you.

The aim of social media was only to connect you with your friends or relatives even you are in any part of the world but today the meaning or use of social media has changed totally. The. Today every teenager wants to expose or explore himself who makes him popular between his friends, collage, school, etc and for that he use the social media where he can do it. Today popularity becomes a big craze for every teenager who makes him different from others youngsters and for get it they take the help of social media today which is the best way for them to become popular but sometimes they do some mistakes on it which becomes a danger for them. The problem is t "we don't know how to use social media actually" but now we need to know if we want to make us secure or safe. In the next topic I have given some tips which makes your life secure while using social media. These all tips are those which actually we need to use but we are using it in totally different way which can become a trouble for us. I only want to say about the "social media" that if you use it carefully then you are safe otherwise there are so many harfmul effects of it which can destroy your personal life forever.

➢ Uploading of photos

Second use is "uploading of photos" which everyone love to do because by this you can show your personality to someone and when you use the social media then the aim of it is totally different as I think because on social media their ae 95% of teenagers are those who share their photos for only show their fun, personallity, activities, etc to others even they strangers or not. But today the craze of photos is increasing day by day in every teenager. Today every teenager wants to become popular between friends or community and for this they use this method because by uploading the photos they can see others that how much they cool or stylish actually. I have given this topic is for explain to you that the activity of upllading photos on social media websites which you do is very risky for everyone which can become a trouble for you. I understand you that how it is risky because it is important to know for everyone and I am sure that after read this topic you will be understand that how a photo can become a trouble for you.

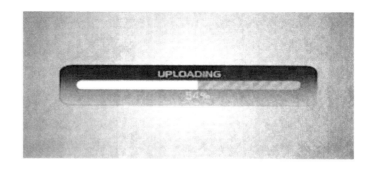

Let's think what is the main fact for which we upload our photos on web and the answer of this question is definitely "for become cool or stylish between friends" but do you know that an attacker can also use your photo as a privcy of him and he can do anything with that. I am saying about it because today it is going on a lot of and in teenagers also this activity is going on. Sometime teenagers perform this type of any activity with someone's photo when they get heart by someone and this is the reality which you can see in your area or neighbour that how a teenager gets heart on web very easily and for revenge he takes a danger step like for misusing of photos. There is also a fact which is "editing" and it is used by 98% teenagers today for making their photos cool or stylish and sometime's some teenagers edit someone's photos illegally without taking his permission and upload it on the web but they don't know that this activity can send them into jail very easily. It's a cyber crime to upload or edit someone's photo on web without taking his permission and if you find into it the you will be in jail with minimum 3 lakh penalty. So don't think that it just like a fun because your fun can become your fear when you get into any trouble because of it. Uploading of photos is not bad but the topic is how you use it which you need to be understand. On social media today the craze of photo upload is increasing day by day in teenagers for which they upload their so many photos in a day for show their personality to others. But where their friends are on web there the attackers are also and it may be that any attacker is your friend on your social media which is waiting for attack on you and you give the chance to him by upload of yor photo because he can misuse of your photo which will be very disappointed for you everytime. You should be know that once you have mistaked ever then that mistake will effect on your whole life. Here below I have given some activities which used by attacker or teenager generally today for take revenge from someone's by upload their photos or misusing of them.

- ✓ They share their bad photos on web which got cheap for all.
- ✓ Click someone's bad activity and upload that on the web for show all.
- ✓ Editing of someone's photo without taking his permission and upload that photo between all friends on web.
- ✓ Uploading someone's photo on any illegal website.

These are some activities which perform by most of teenagers today for revenge with someone's because they know that on web if anyone's got expose then it will be a very insulting for him so they perform these type of activities and they don't care about the result of it that what will be happen because they got crazy while doing this and can't see or understand anything by which they perform some wrong activities on web. I want to understand you that what can be happen and whats the effect it will on your life if you perform any wrong activity on web even it's uploading of photos or other. So, always be smart while uploading any photo on web because here are so many people who don't care about someone's emotions and can perform any type of activity even it will wrong or right. You should be understand the advantages or disadvanatages of web where you are depending day by day and spend your life on it between 90% strangers who are unknown. You should be remember one thing always while using internet that is "internet is not your life and a lot of part of it is fake only so don't be crazy for it or depend on it because it just like a magical room which have the only entrance door not exit door where you can come very easily but to leave it is very difficult for everyone". So be careful and don't share or upload your photos with your friends which are not close to you and never talk with any stranger or give him your personal information.

➢ Chatting or Messaging:

Now let's come to the next point and that is "Chatting" or "Messaging" which become very popular between teenagers and I think that there is no any teenager may be which don't know about "chatting" or not using it because today every teenager has the mobile phone generally and the fact is that it will be the smartphone a lot of time. So, if they have the smartphone then definitely they handle it with smartly like playing games, using applications, surfing or browsing, downloading and a lot of work in which one of the best use is only the "chatting" or "messaging" and you can see the examplein your real life that how the teenagers use the smartphones and what they do with that generally and you will find that they generally use the phone for chat.

Today it become so easy to chat with someone because of social media or other messaging applications by which we can chat and it is very intresting to chat with someone because we make it's a fun for us. Because of social networking websites we can chat with strangers also from any part of the world and make them friends but is it right to use it in this way? As you know that on social network anybody can meet you or join you and you can easily make friend with him but the topic is that should we do it or not ? It just like a fun for us but actually it is a problem for us. You can take a example for your real life also that when you use the socail network where you have so many unknown friends and you chat them without knowing their privacy or information. You don't know also that is that person a male or female who is chatting with you even he wrote "female or male" on his privacy but the truth is totally different. It means that we only chat with someone to make fun or timepaas even we know him or not. We don't care anything while we chat with someone. I only want to understand you that the person from which you are chatting can be a criminal also who can harm you on web by gaining your personal information from you. Chatting means to communicate with someone if you are not with him or her but we use it with a wrong way in which we chat with strangers which are unknonwn always. Most of teenagers do this mistake and sometime they got webbed and get into the trouble which effects on their lifes. You should be understand that on web 90% people are unknown or stranger for you in which some people are those who want to make harm others and for that they make you friends and gain your information then leak it on web. When you chat on web you don't see the person behind the chat so it can be anyone even it can be a criminal aslo. So you should be careful always when somebody chat with you and the best prevention for it is only that don't make friends on web who are unknown or stranger and always chat with your relatives, friends or known members. If you follow this then you will be secure otherwise anyone can cheat you very easily on web. Here are some important points which you should be check or remember for chat someone on web.

- ✓ If the person is unknown or he has no any mutual friend then stop chat with him.
- ✓ Chat with those people who are known only generally.
- ✓ whenever you dought while chat with someone then immediately first checkup the person's profile.
- ✓ If any unknown gives you any unknown link while chat then immediately delete it and unfriend that person.

➢ Sharing

As you know that today every teenagers have a smartphone generally in which they have a lot of intresting things which they show to others or share with them like applications, data, photos, games, music, etc. Here I am saying about sharing of data photos, music, etc which also become a craze today for every teenager and they use it everytime whenever they are in between of friends. Sharing is one and only service which is used by everyone today but the problem is that they use it anywhere.

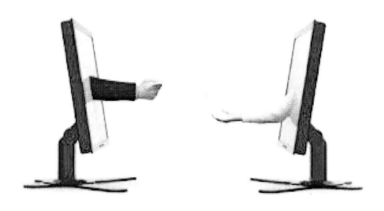

Most of teenagers think that sharing is a secure method to send any data someone but they are wrong actually because there is no anything in technology which has no any problem. I want to tell somehing about sharing that is when you share anything then its go through air which means we can get it if we captured it so attackers can easily get your data whatever you shared with someone. I am telling this for understand you that you use sharing anywhere without any fear but you should not be do this generally. You know that when we share anything by bluetooth then it goes through air but do you know that if anyone sniff that data then he can easily get that data and steal it. Here are some tips which you should be remember always when you share anything with bluetooth or any other device.

✓ **While share anything always check that is there any extra device get connected** with you or not and if it then immediately disconnect it.

✓ Never pair any device while sharing because after pairing your device will be acceptable for searching of files or directories.

✓ Do not use any speical or untrusted application for sharing any data because it can be a trojan also.

So, always remember these tips while sharing your data with someone's because anybody can steal it if you not secure it and you can imagine that what will happen if your data get steal or leak.

How to use social media ?

Every teenager thinks that social media is a very intresting way to make fun and because of only it he use. But he don't know that he is not playing with his own life while using social media because today the meaning of social media becomes totally different for 90% of teenagers and that's why they use it only for make fun and sometimes they webbed because of their mistakes which they perform on social media. In this topic you will get the tips that how you should be use the social media and remember that all the tips are very important because they all relates with your social life so follow them if you want to become safe while using social media otherwise the choice is your's.

➢ Don't allow anyone to use your account

I have seen a lot of time that most of teenagers are those who us their friends gadegts to operate their accounts or allow their friends to use their account but I would like to suggest you all that never do it because as I think today every teenager has very aggressive mind even he is your friend or not. So, whenever he used your account for illegaly or misusing then you will be get into trouble which can get you into the jail. I only want to say that never share your account with your friends or others

➢ Never share your details with someone

When you use social media then it becomes your personal life book which contains your all secrets or important details and you don't want to share them with someone. But today in this age of teenagers there are so many teenagers who want to expose them sociallyon the web and for that they share their personal or important details with their friends or others but the fact is that they think that it is very intresting but they don't know that they are mistaking and become a very big fool. Because if someone's get your details then he has all about you which he can use illegaly or any other purpose and which will be get trouble for you and affect your life. So, remember always that never share your any personal information or details with someone's even they are your friends or relatives. Today everyone want to know the secrets of others life and most of people specialy teenagers do this mistake by using social media for sharing their details, secrets, data, etc.

➢ Never chat with stranger

Social media connects everone to each other and 98% people use it for make friends because here they can do it very easily and make their friends from any part of the world even they know that they all are the strangers for them but this is intresting and sometime this intrest become a big trouble for them. Those people whose you don't know or meet ever known is "Stranger" which means that it can be anyone even its your friend of any attacker but you can't be understand them on web because it is very easy to hide your privacy on web and by using it most of attackers attack on you while you use social media. Today 97% are those people on the social media who are using it for make friends or connect others even they are strangers or not. I only want to say that never add any stranger person in your account or chat with him because it can be any attacker who can makes you harm.

➢ Never share your photo with someone

I have seen that 70% people share their personal photos with someone's on social media while chatting. I want to inform those all that please don't do this because anyone can misuse your photo on web and you can't do anything if he peroforms any activity on your photo. I specially want to inform all the girls who use social media and share their photos with someone that don't do it because it can be harm you on web.

➢ Do not use any fake profile

If you are using any fake profile for making fool others then stop it now because it is a fun for you but actually you don't know that you are doing a crime which will send you into jail very easily. This type of activity is perform by most of teenagers today because they want to make fool their friends or others for test them or get their secrets or information but they don't know that it is illegal and crime. If anyone reports against you then you will be in jail with a high penalty. So, always remember before to do this type of any activity on web because your one mistake can become a big trouble for you.

➢ Do not post any wrong thing

Most of teenagers use fake profiles and by that profile they post or upload any wrong matter or photo which is illegal or persoanl. They should not be do this because it will be get them into a very big trouble. While doing this type of activity you think that nothing will happen but if anyone reports you once then you will be arrest and go to jail. So, think always before upload or post anything on web or social media because here everything is dangerous.

➢ Do not abuse someone

On social media nobody can see you actual privacy that who are you? And because of this sometimes you do mistakes. While chatting or posting sometime's you abuse someone privately and you think that he can't get you or see you so without any fear you abusing him but you know that if that person reports against you then you will find into the cyber crime and for that you will go to the jail. So, always remember that it is not neccessory to see you all time whenever you chat and that's why you abuse because if someone reports against you then you will be bang very easily.

Crimes on Social Media

Everyone is using social media today as we know in which their are most of teenagers. Social media websites begins a craze in every teenager which attracts him towards it by which he get crazy for use it. You can see in your neighbour that how teenagers become crazy for social media and spend their a lot of time on it because its one and only the best service on which they can make fun a lot. Whenever we talk about the social media then always the name which we use is one and only "facebook". Facebook is a social networking website which used by 90% teenageres today all over the country and it becomes most popular because of its features which given below as you can see:

✓ Uploading your photos and videos.
✓ Share anything with your friends.
✓ Make friends from anywhere of the world.

- ✓ Get connected everytime with your friends or relatives.
- ✓ Post your updates betweenyour friends.

As you can understand from the above points that how is it intresting for everyone. Here we are talk about the teenagers who are most users of it today and spend their a lot of time on it and perform a lot of activities in a day in which uploading of photos, videos, post, comment, sharing, etc contains. But the way which we are using for it is that correct or not? I am asking this question to you because we all perform these activities and between us there are some people who use these types of activities for misusing or abusing someone. I think that it's a very serious problem between teenagers that they don't care about anything while they use internet even it right or wrong. But now you should be think about it because 40% of teenagers use social media to insult or abuse someone only you know. They do the 8crime actually by doing this type of any activity because its not a small topic to abuse someone which can heart him.

Some teenagers do this for only take the revenge from someone but most of them use it for only their fun because they think that it is so cool to do these type of activites between their friends or others and actually they don't know that they are doing crime which can send them into jail very easily.I have seen so many cases in which teenagers reports only for cyber abusing in which someone has been abused them personally or socially on web and you know the most of cases are from social media like facebook because it is used by everyone and only because of its smart services or features it is very easy to abuse somone on it. Here are some activities which some teenagers perform on social media and it can make a criminal to them by which they get into the jail easily.

- ✓ Uploading of 18+ images on social media between friends or others.
- ✓ Share some important information of someone with others.
- ✓ Post any wrong thing on someone's profile without any permission.
- ✓ Share any wrong thing with others like videos or photos.
- ✓ Using of fake profile and make fool others.

These are some activities which perform by some teenagers generally on social media and they think that nothing will happen with them because nobody can do anything. But actually they are wrong basically because its a crime and if anyine reports against them then easily they go into the jail with heavy charges. Whenever I saw these type of cases then mostly I have seen that in most of cases their are girls be a victim who got abused by somone's on web. Girls upload their photos on web which used by attackers for abuse them and by using that photos they can easily insult the girls on web. So, never upload your personal photos on web and this is specially for the girls who always do this. Here is the another activity which is used by teenagers a lot today and that is one and only uploading of photos with editing even they will be themselves or others. But do you know that it is a cyber crime which is known as the "morphing". In which you edit someone photo with other photo and change that photo completely with other. This is used by attackers generally for abusing someone photo by changing that with any wrong photo and this is generally performed on girls mostly. I want to tell you that the method you use this is generally a crime but if you misuse it otherwise it's not a crime to upload your own photo by editing. I am saying this to inform you all that never put up your real photos on social media and never share them with any unknown person because it could be any attacker. So, you need to be smart while using social media because here you are playing with criminal activities and your one wrong step can send you in jail.

Life of teenagers on Internet

Now let's have a tour of today's teenager life which they spend on internet. 98% teenagers are those who spend their whole day on internet specialy in chatting and sharing as I think. It just like a craze which attracts them always towards it. There are so many parts of this life and each part has its own property and function. But is it right to use it a lot? Obvisouly the answer is no always. Because where internet has advantages then it also has a lot of disadvantages. It depends on you that how you use it as a advantage or disadvantage? Because every step of your's is very important to notice otherwise in the world of Internet you will loose your private life within few minute. The most important topic is that what are the disadvantages of internet by which most of teenagers got webbed because internet is like a tricky world and here most of people are only for cheat you so be careful while using it.

➢ No privacy

As we know that everyone has its own privacy which he don't like to share with someone because he has some secrets or any important detail about him which he don't want to share. We can say them "secret person" because they hides their secrets from everyone. This is the most important topic for every teenager of today because you can notice also that 90% teenagers don't like to share their privacy with friends, family members or others because they don't want to explore it. But today this is not going on because in these 90% teenagers want to explore them or their privacy with everyone which makes them popular from others in their collages, schools, community, etc and the best way for it the one and only using of social media and today it has become a important part of every teenager in their life.

Every teenager wants to expose himself between his friends today but sometimes he do any mistake which becomes a danger for him and only because of that mistake his life get totally destroy. In this topic we will discuss that how the most of teenagers get into a danger because of their one mistake to explore on social media. Here we are talking about the privacy that is important for everyone and if someone privacy get steal then it means his all important information, details, secrets will be expose between the locality. But today teenagers don't care about it because they are in craze in which they explores them between the whole world by using social media but they don't know actually that they are mistaking which will get them into a large trouble. Here is the list of mistakes which performs by 90% teenagers today on social media websitesand they can make effect in their life and get into them in a big trouble:

✓ **Sharing of personal details with everyone on social media like personal name, address, phone number, etc.**

- ✓ They share their all live activity on social media.
- ✓ Most of these share their origional photographs with strangers.
- ✓ Share personal details with someones or strangers.
- ✓ Make trust on someone which will be the stranger actually.
- ✓ Share their secrets with the whole world on social media.

So, these are some most activities which teenagers perform on social media today and they think that it is cool but they don't know the reality that what would be happen with them because of these type of mistakes which they do on social media without any limit.

➢ No Limit

Internet is a fun for most of teenagers because here they have the freedom to do anything without any limit and sometime because of it they do mistakes which become trouble for them. They think that on Internet nobody can see them that what are they doing so that's why sometimes they take some dangerous steps on Internet which get them into a large trouble. As you know that on Internet you can do anything which is like a fun for you and you also do it but do you know that you are wrong actually that nobody can see you. I want to tell something to those teenagers who think that nobody can see their activities which they do on Internet so you should be know that your whole activity is being recorded everytime whatever you perform on Internet.

Internet has no limit but it doesn't mean that you can do anything here even it's right or wrong because Internet is a web where you can easily be trapped yourself because of your one small mistake. Today, every teenager wants to do different from others and when he is on Internet then his craze get increase and sometimes he perform some serious activity because of it which becomes a problem for him and his life get totally effected. You shoulb be understand the reality behind Internet if you use it because on

Internet your every step is risky which can be change into a big problem ever if you do not point that. So, when you are on Internet then always think before to perform any activity on it. Here are some activities which perform by most of teenagers today on Internet without any limit and sometimes they get into trouble because of them also.

- ✓ Video chat with someone even he is stranger or not.
- ✓ Abusing someone on web.
- ✓ Sharing of someone secrets with others.
- ✓ Uploading of shameful videos on Internet.
- ✓ Blackmailing someone online on Internet.

So, these are some activities which perfrom by so many teenagers and sometime the result of these type of activites is very dangerous for which they can be into jail. By using these type of activities against someone on Internet you destroy the both of lifes you and him totally. So remember, Internet is not for fun because here every step of you is so risky for everyone which can be effect on your whole life totally.

➤ No Rules

Have you think ever that what is the main thing which makes every teenager crazy for the internet and they can't live without it? If not then think now because it's very important to know for all of us. This happens because every teenager has its own thinking when he use the internet because here they can do anyhthing.Their is no any special rules which stops them to do anything and they make a lot of fun which gives enjoy to them. Whenever they use internet then they think that there is no any teacher who is observing them or teaching them so they can do anything here with independence. This topic is very important to understand for every parent if their children are using internet a lot of because if there is no rule here then they can do a lot of things in which some can be dangerous or serious for them which they don't know actually and get them into any trouble. Here are some dangers given below by which you can be into any problem ever if you don't know them because if there is no rule for you on internet then also attacker has the same by which he can attacks on you and grab you into his trap.

- ✓ **Never access any unknown link which sends by someone who is unknown.**
- ✓ **If you get any serious message then immediately inform to cyber shell of your area.**
- ✓ **Never put up your any information on any untrusted website.**

➤ Access of unknown websites

Have you know that why most of teenagers use the internet a lot of? If no then the answer of this question is very simple and that is only "the internet has some intrested websites and services for which they use it a lot". Websites make the teenagaers crazy for use the internet because website is only a way to make fun on internet and as you know that there are so many types of websites are available on internet which are amazing and intresting because of we get attracr towards them and become crazy for access them. Websites have some attractive matters which attracts the users to use it and whenever any user use it then he got crazy and want to use it again and again.Today we access so many websites in a day on internet in which every website is different from others. But the question is here that "how they effects on teenagers?". Because today every teenager use the internet where he access the so many websites of different types and sometime's he gets attract towards any wrong website which get him into any problem from where it is very difficult to leave You can understand that what I want to say. I mean to say only that today the craze of internet makes the teenagers crazy for it and sometimes they get into the problem because of their craze in which most of teenagers are those who get into the problem because of accessing on unknown or wrong websites only. There are so many websites present on internet which attracts you towards them and you easily get attract even you know them or not. It is a very serious problem for children who use the internet because there are so many unknown websites available on internet in which also the adult websites are and they access them sometime's which they should not to do and once they access them then they totally attract towards it and become crazy for these types of websites. Here are some effects given below which change yourself because of access unkown websites only.

- ✓ These websites change your mentality totally on internet.
- ✓ You can't leave the craze of it very easily if you get into it once.
- ✓ These types of websites change your thinking sense generally.
- ✓ Some of websites are those who gives you money for your work online and sometimes you get into it

which makes you fool completely and cheat you.

✓ **These websites attracts you towards them and creates the serious problems for you online.**

So, be careful while using internet and never access any unknown website which you don't know becausee it can easily effect on your life which will change your thinking. You need to use ite internet only for help not to make fun.

Children vs Internet

Internet is a magical world which looks good from outer but whenever you get into it then you can't be leave it because the attraction of internet is very strong which always try to attract you from towards it but the choice is yours that are you attract or not. You know that how the users of internet is increasing day by day and most of the users are teenagers who are using internet. Have you think ever that what is the correct age for us to use the internet. If your answer is no then please think now because it is a very serious matter for all of us because most of children are also using the internet even they are in the age of teenager or not. I am talking this because today's children are so exciting to use eeverything which they see and internet is one and only the first thing which they all see in their homes, schools, etc and then they want to use it. The problem is not that they want to use it but the problem is that they want to use it in a very little age in which they should not be use it because as I told that internet is very attractive which always attracts you towards it so if the children get attract towards it then it will effects on thier both of life and mind. Sometimes children become crazy for internet because they know that here they can do a lot of intresting things which makes fun but they don't think that what will the result of this if they use it a lot of. I think that we should not give the internet service to any children if he is not under 18 because you know that on internet their are so many services are those who attracts you a lot of towards it and these all are very risky for everyone so we need to understand this serious topic and never should be give the access of internet to any children. Here are some services of internet given below which can effects on children mind and life if they use it or attract towards it.

✓ **On internet there are so many type of unknown websites which are risky and attracts to everyone towards them.**

✓ **Advertisements of 18+ services are here on which so many children get attract.**

✓ **Anybody can make fool them and make them cyber bulling very easily.**

✓ **There are so many websites for chat which attracts the children a lot.**

✓ **While using internet children get connected with some adult websites which they should be access.**

✓ **Misusing of internet for uploading, watching, sharing any bad things on internet.**

You can understand easily from the above that what I would like to say about internet and children that how Internet can effect on children and you can see in your locality for a live example that every children even he is 10 years old or 15 years old knows about the internet and also know to operate it. Its a very serious topic for parents whose children is using internet in the age of 10-16 years because in this age the mind of every child is creative and internet can easily divert it which will effect on them so you need to care your children at this age specialy if they are using internet. You need to check everytime that what they are doing on internet because it is very important to do. Here are some tips given below which is very important for every parent to follow their children if they are using internet.

- ✓ **First block every unknown or 18+ website from your network immediately.**
- ✓ **Only enable the education websites onyour system by which no any extra website get access.**
- ✓ **Always lookup your children everytime while they surf on web that what they are searching on it.**

✓ **Disable the advertisements on your system by which no any unwanted or 18+ advertisement will come.**
✓ **Never give permission to your child for using the internet connection without you.**

So, these are some best ways to stay away your children from the internet web and these will definately help you. Always remember that internet is a very risky place where your every step is risky which can get you in any problem. So, the responsibility for children future is ours and for this we need to take care them while they use internet because in this age they get attract towards anything very easily so be careful because this is not the age of them to do this type of activities which can destroy their life forever. Now the duty is yours that how you care your children and stay away them from the internet always and never use the internet in front of them because if you do this then they will follow you definately and use it.

Advantages or Disadvantages

As you know that everything has two parts in which one is good another is bad always and the choice is ours that what we choose. Here, I am talking about the internet which is our life today because we all spend our whole day on it even we are teenager or not. Internet is using by everyone today and it is like a best friend for teenagers which can do anything. But as I sai that everything has two parts so the internet has also be good or bad and this is very important for us to know the both of parts because if internet can help us then it can also be destroy our life forever if we get into any problem here. So, you must be need to understand the both of advantages and disadvantages of Internet. When internet had invented then the developers think that it will help others but today the meaning of internet is totally different and it become more dangerous then helpful but it depends upon us that how we use it because if it has disadvantages then it has also the advantages which can help us ad makes our life easy. In this topic we will know about the advantages and disadvantages of Internet. In previous topics we have learnt that how the teenagers get into problem, become criminals, about their craze, etc on internet but now we will read that what the internet can do and how it can be useful or dangerous for us if we don't use it in a correct way because if we use it then we should be know about it. Now first we read about the advantages of Internet that what we can do with internet and how it can be useful for us and makes our life so easy and comfortable.

Internet is use by everyone today but the difference is only that some people use it as a help and some sue it as a danger and here we are talking about the advantages of it which makes our life comfortable and easy. Advantages means those type of ways which helps us in our work and makes us comfortable. Some advantages of internet has been given below which we generally use in our daily life very easily because of internet.

✓ We can easily send our messages to anyone within few seconds through internet.

✓ We can communicate with our family members from any part of world.

✓ We can pay our bills from anywhere through internet.

✓ We can study from internet and get any type of information in few minutes.

So these are the some advantages of internet which help us in our daily life and we all know about it because we all use it. Now the question comes here that "are we really use the internet for these types of work today" because the attraction of internet is like a wine which makes us crazy for it and once we get into it then it is very difficult to leave it as you know that and sometimes because of this craze we also get into any problem. Previous we read about the advantages of internet and now we read about the disadvantages of internet which use by a lot of teenagers today because they think that it's for fun but actually they are playing with a danger which result will be dangerous. Today everyone is on internet we all know that and specially there are 90% of teenagers from those people who are using internet. Most of teenagers use it for only make fun but the topic is that they use the disadvantages of internet which they think as the fun for them and sometimes this fun becomes a big trouble for them in which they can't be leave out very easily. Here I have given the disadvantages of internet which teenagers use as a fun but now read them and think that are you right or wrong? and see that what are you doing with internet and what can it do with your life.

- ✓ Sharing our all live activity with others on social networking websites.
- ✓ Follow the bad things on Internet which get ban for us.
- ✓ See or upload the 18+ videos or photos on web and share them with others.
- ✓ Abusing or blackmailing someone on web throught his photos or videos.
- ✓ Performing of shamefull activities on web which actually we should not to do ever.

So, you can understand from the above activites that what you do sometime through internet and how they can effect on your life and not only this it can make you a criminal also because this is a crime to play with someone's feelings on web which send you in jail easily so always remember that internet is not for the fun because it can makes your lie easy so it can also destroy it.

How teen become a criminal

Today, the best friend of teenagers is one and only "internet" as we know because they spend their lot of time on it. They have made it their life where they want only fun. But the internet life is like a open book of any personal life which has no privacy so anyone can read it and because of this sometimes teenagers get into the problem. Teenagers get crazy while using internet and then they don't care about anything that what they are doing on it. They think everything is like a fun nut actually they are wrong and sometimes this fun become a big trouble for them from which they can't be get out easily. Where internet is a medium for make fun there it is also a medium for doing crime and this is true that most of teenagers got attacked by internet on their personal or private lifes. The most important thing about it that is whenever any teenager got webbed or attacked then it effects on his whole life and sometimes they do not tolerate that. If you use the internet then you should be know about the both of profit and loss which you get from the internet because here anybody can makes you fool and cheat you. I am talking about this because most of teenagers do this mistakes on internet because of their craze and after sometime they get cheat by someone.

Now let's talk about the most important topic about teenagers that is "how the teenagers

become a criminal on internet sometimes ".
Yeah!! This is true that sometimes a teenager
becomes a criminal because of his craze on
internet. But before strating the topic first see
what are the ways below because of teenagers
become a criminal on internet.

✓ **When they get cheat by someone's
    on internet then they perform the
    activity which makes them criminal.**
✓ **For take revenge from someone's
    they follow the criminal type
    activites on web.**
✓ **By misusing of someone's images
    on web they become criminals.**
✓ **For insulting someone's in between
    of people they perform activities on
    web.**
✓ **For cheating with someone's on
    web.**

So, these are some activities which perform by
the teenagers sometimes and because of these
they become a criminal easily on web. Today's
teenagers are so agressive and because of this

they don't want to compromise with others and whenever they get hert by someone's then they want to take revenge from that person for which they use the internet because on internet it is very easy to insult someone. Most of teenagers perform these type of activites today for insulting someone through web and this is like a fun for them for which they don't care about anything and sometimes they get into a big problem because of it and go into the jail and known as a criminal. In social networking websites these type of activites are perform by teenagers a lot of as I seen because social media is used by every teenager today where they share their social life with others even they known or not. Now the question comes here that why teenagers perform these type of activities against someone's by which both of lifes can be destroy as they know but they do this and the result of it is very dangerous you know because it is not easy to tolerating of insult between the whole world. Teengaers think that by do this type of any activity they can easily take the revenge from someone but they don't think about the result of it which will be very effective. They do this for make fun only as they think but actually this is not a fun you know also that it's a crime which makes you criminal. Internet is not for insulting, cheating, blackmailing, harassing, etc even it is a very useful for all of us but the choice is yours that how you use it because your one mistake can make you a criminal or destroy your whole life forever.

You can see the private reports that how many teenagers got webbed within a month by which they suicide sometime's because they can't be handle the situation actually in which they get into and this is only because of web. I want to discuss something with all of those teenagers who share their personal feelings, information, photos, details on internet daily for become cool between friends or others then please stop it now because here anybody can cheat you easily. Specially for those girls who upload their photos on web then stop it now and never put up your photos on web because there are so many cases are those in which girls got insulted because of their bad uses with photos. On internet, 60% of cheaters are available only you know who always wait for a chance to make harms you and whenever you get into the contact with them then first they make their trust on you and after sometime they cheat or heart you on web between the whole world and you don't take any action against that. So, what should be do if we get into this type of any problem. Here are the solutions which I have given below:

✓ **If anyone blackmails you on web for any purpose then immediately reprt against him on that website which he is using.**

✓ **If anyone upload your photo without your permission and misuse it then first report against him in cyber shell department of your area then complain on the website** community and delete your photo from that website immediately.

✓ You can report against anyone in the online website community if he cheats, blackmail, hack, abuse, etc you.

Internet as a Weapon

Today where the users of internet is increasing day by day then it becomes easy to attack someone personaly because by using internet attackers can easily make harm you without doing any personal activity. Most of people think that internet is a very useful service for everyone but I think that it's a weapon actually for everyone by which we can easily attack on someone's privacy within few minutes and insult him between the whole world. You know, the attack of internet is more harmful then private because it destroy the whole life on web between the whole world which is the shamefull for everyone who got attacked. But why and how anyone use the internet for attacking someone have you think ever? I think that there are most of teenagers between attackers who use the internet as a weapon for make harm someone because in the world of teenager every teen wants to become popular and cool and don't want to see others become cool or stylish so he use the internet for shame him live between the whole world or friends by using web. Teenagers do not want to compromise with their social life because they got crazy for it and if anyone disturb them for it them they makes their mind to take revenge from him by using web. Here are some activities of teenagers given below in which both boys and girls come who perform these type of activities for take revenge from someone through web which is very risky for everyone because it can destroy the life with shame.

✓ **Blackmailing of someone by using his shameful photo or video.**

- ✓ Sharing of someone's secret videos or photos which he don't want to share with others.
- ✓ Uploading someone's shameful photos on social network.
- ✓ Cheat someone by chatting him with any fake profile.
- ✓ Perform shameful activity on web by using someone's privacy or profile.

You can be easily understand that what can be do with you with these activities which given above because this is the reality which do by a lot of teenagers on web when they want to take revenge from someone because they think that this is the best way to insult someone between others. You know, 20% of teenagers suicide only for stressed or get dippressed because for internet abuse and today it become common for every teenager because they all use the internet so they think that its very easy to make fun with someone and by using web they do this but after that the result is so dangerous for both of them because sometime's their fun become a big problem for them from which it is difficult to get out. It is very easy to use internet but its so difficult to understand it because it has so many types and each type is different from others which has their own advantages and dis-advantages.I only want to say that never use the internet for perform any wrong activity on internet because your one mistake can destroy your life online forever. This is not a joke, you are playing with your life while using internet because your one wrong step can send you in jail very easily. So, always think first to take any step on internet that what are you doing and is that right or wrong. You need to know the use of internet in your life if you use it and you also need to tell others about it because it is very important to introduce others with the reality of internet which get hidden behind it and don't see us by which sometimes we get into the problem.

Teenagers war on internet

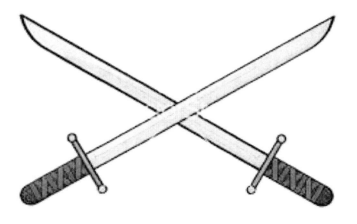

As we know that today every teenager use the internet for lot of work in which 90% of teenagers use it for make the fun only and because of it they got crazy for it ad spend their whole time on it even they are on computers or mobile phones. It becomes their life where they don't have any rule which means they can do anything but sometimes they use it with a very big craze which get them into problem. Every teenager wants to exposehimself on internet for which he can do anything and if anyone disturbs him then he makes angry and wants to take revenge from him for which sometime he use the way of crime through internet which is the fun for him but atucally its not fun, its a war. Sometimes, teenager takes some most dangerous steps on internet becauss of their internet craze which get them into a big problem forever from which it is very difficult to leave for them. You do not have any idea yet that what could be happen when any teenager takes the wrong step on internet because that one step of him will effect on his life which is the very serious problem for everyone. Teenagers never think that what they are doing on internet because they are in craze of it and thats why they do some serious mistakes .Today every teen has been depended on internet because internet is like a best friend for him which always give fun to him without any limit and thats why they don't want to leave it never and sometimes this craze has been changed into a live war in which one teenager wants to shame others from whose he want to take revenge and you can understand that how he goes into a wrong way by doing this type of activity because this is very dangerous or serious for both of teenagers who are attacker and victim. Here are some activites of teenagers given below which they perform generally for take revenge from someone through internet.

- ✓ Cheating someone by using any fake profile on social media.
- ✓ Leaking of someone mms on web for insulting him between the whole world.
- ✓ Hacking into someone's profile and perform any shameful activity to insult him on web.
- ✓ Bad use of someone's photos by editing and upload them on web between all of friends.
- ✓ Uploading of shameful photos or videos online.

- ✓ Perform some shameful activities between all over the friends live on web.
- ✓ Live video calling with shameful activities.
- ✓ Making fool someone and heart him online between all over the friends.
- ✓ Misuse someone photos with illegal activites on web.

I am telling these all activities for inform you that how teenagers get into the problem while using internet and once they got grabbed then it is very difficult for them to leave it or share that with somone because it's shamefull for them so they can't share it with others and sometimes this becomes a very serious problem for them by which they get depressed and suicide. Every teenager has a exposive mind today which one use the internet so he don't want that someone cheats him but whenever they got cheat the they take their revenge through internet which is so dangerous. I want to inform those all teenagers who use the internet and also have this type of any idea to take revenge from someone then please stop it now because it will destroy your life seriously because after this you will become a criminal within few seconds and go into the jail. Not only this you heart others for doing this type of activity because nobody wants to insult themselves live on web between others so if anybody insult someone then it is very difficult to understand the situation. You should be understand the side effects of internet which attracts you towards them always whenever you are on the internet because there is a large number of disadvantages of internet more then its advantages. Only the choice is yours when you use it then what you choose and what you perform because each step can destroy your social life forever on web very easily.You should not be take any step on internet which is risky or which hearts others because the result of this step will be very dangerous for you. Internet is not a weapon friends which you use to take revenge from others. Its a helpful service for all of us where we can get any type of help but the problem is that we don't want to understand it in a correct way because we love to make fun with it even we know that this is very dangerous and risky for us. You know that today most of teenagers suicide for the cause of cyber abuse only because they don't have the power to handle the situtaion in which they be. They don't care about their parents that what will be with them if they not with them. I want to say only that todays teenagers are not so strong which can handle any serious situation and because of internet whenever they get webbed then they can't understand that what they should be do and they takes the wrong step which is only "suicide". So, never hearts or insult anyone on internet because your fun can destroy someone's life very easily and it will also effect on your life and you will not get the chance for get out from it.

Helpful tips for you

Everyone who is using internet today and spend his all time on it for make fun only then this is a very important topic for him because your fun is a danger whichh you don't understand actually and when you understand it then the time has been gone for you. So, here in this topic you will get a lot of important tips or countermeasures for you that what should be do on internet and what shouldn't. All the tips are very important to follow because it's a very serious matter for all of us which we think as a fun and sometime's this fun makes us criminal or disappointed. Here I have given the whole tips in this topic which presented in the whole book. Now first we read that what we never should to do on internet which can become a problem for us or get us into any trouble.

❖ **If you are chatting with any stranger person on web then stop it immediately because it could be any attacker or ciminal which can harms** you on internet by using your information.

❖ Never use any unauthorized website because it can be hack you by that website and easily steal your whole personal and important information.

❖ If you are using any social networking website then never get connected with any unknown person which has any fake profile and you don't know him personally

❖ Never upload your photo on your profile if you have unknown friends and this is specially for the girls because most of girls do this and after they got webbed.

❖ If you receive any unknown email on your account then you should be report for that immediately in cyber shell of your area.

❖ Do not share any information with your friends or others on social media because they can use it for any illegal purpose also.

❖ Never create any fake account on web for make fool others because it's a crime and you can be send yourself into jail very easily.

❖ Never access any website from any advertisements because it could be any spoofer or sniffer which transfers your all information to the criminal or attacker.

So, these are some important tips which you need to remember always while using internet. You should be follow these all tips always while using internet becaue its very important or serious for everyone to know otherwise anybody can cheat you on internet and use yourself as a profit of him. Now let's talk about the countermeasures which everybody should be remember whenever they get into any big problem on internet. These are those problems in which most of people got trapped on web and this is a very serious problem for everyone because most of people get into it but they don't knoe that how to solve it. So, that's why I have given some countermeasures for a lot of problems in which you generally trap live while using internet.

❖ **If anybody cheats or abuse you on web then you can register your report against him/her in cyber shell of your area or that community.**

❖ **If anybody sends you any untrusted link in your inbox then immediately delete that message.**

❖ For block unwanted messages on youer account you can use any strong firewall which have some services like these which will block the unwanted or spam messages or emails automatically.

❖ You need to enable your pop-up blocker always which will block the phishing or untrusted websites automatically from your web browser.

❖ Never do any transaction or payment through any untrusted or unauthorized website.

Cybercrime cells in India

Here are the listof cyber crime cells has been given with their complete contants and addresses for those people who don't know that where they can submit their reports against cyber crime. I want to say you all that if you got webbed then please report for it in your cyber crime cell department of your area and don't be silent because if you be silent then attackers become so powerful and they will attack again on others.

➤ Chennai

Address: Asst. Commr. of Police,

Cyber Crimes Cell, Vepery, Chennai 7

Contact Details: 04423452348, 04423452350

E-mail id: cybercrimechn@yahoo.com

➢ For Rest of Tamil Nadu,

Address: A-Wing, III rd Floor,

Rajaji Bhawan, Besant Nagar, Chennai-600090

ph: 044-24461959, 24468889,24463888

E-mail id: hobeochn@cbi.gov.in

➢ Bangalore

(for whole of the Karnataka)

Address: Cyber Crime Police Station

C.O.D Headquarters, Carlton House, # 1, Palace Road, Bangalore - 560 001

Contact Details: +91-80-2220 1026 ,+91-80-2294 3050 Website: http://www.cyberpolicebangalore.nic.in /

➤ Hyderabad

Address: Cyber Crime Police Station, Crime Investigation Department,

3rd Floor, D.G.P. office, Lakdikapool, Hyderabad – 500004

Contact Details: +91-40-2324 0663, +91-40-2785 2274

Website:http://www.cidap.gov.in/cybercrimes.aspx

E-mail id: cidap@cidap.gov.in, info@cidap.gov.in

➤ Delhi

CBI Cyber Crime Cell:

Superintendent of Police,

Cyber Crime Investigation Cell

Central Bureau of Investigation,

5th Floor, Block No.3,

CGO Complex, Lodhi Road, New Delhi – 3

Contact Details: +91-11-4362203, 011-26851998, 011-26515229, +91-11-4392424

Web site: http://cbi.nic.in/

➢ Thane

Address: 3rd Floor, Police Commissioner Office

Near Court Naka, Thane West, Thane 400601.

Contact Details: +91-22-25424444

Web site: www.thanepolice.org

E-Mail: police@thanepolice.org

➤ Pune

Deputy Commissioner of Police(Crime)

Office of the Commissioner Office, 2, Sadhu Vaswani Road,

Camp,Pune 411001

Contact Details: +91-20-26123346, +91-20-26127277

+91-20-2616 5396, +91-20-2612 8105 (Fax)

E-Mail: crimecomp.pune@nic.in, punepolice@vsnl.com

➤ Gujarat

DIG, CID, Crime and Railways, Fifth Floor, Police Bhavan

Sector 18, Gandhinagar 382 018

Contact Details: +91-79-2325 4384, +91-79-2325 0798

➤ Jharkhand

IG-CID,Organized Crime

Rajarani Building,Doranda Ranchi, 834002

Ph: +91-651-2400 737/ 738

➤ Mumbai

Address: Cyber Crime Investigation Cell, Office of Commissioner of , Police office,Annex -3 Building,

1st floor, Near Crawford Market, Mumbai-01.

Contact Details: +91-22-22630829, +91-22-22641261

E-mail id: officer@cybercellmumbai.com

➤ Himachal Pradesh

CID Office , Dy.SP, Himachal Pradesh

Contact Details: +91-94180 39449

E-mail:soodbrijesh9@gmail.com

➤ Haryana

Cyber Crime and Technical Investigation Cell,

Joint Commisioner of Police

Old S.P.Office complex,Civil Lines, Gurgaon

E-mail: jtcp.ggn@hry.nic.in

➢ Jammu

SSP,Crime, CPO Complex,Panjtirthi, Jammu-180004

Contact Details : +91-191-257-8901

E-mail: sspcrmjmu-jk@nic.in

➢ Kerala

Hitech Cell, Police Head Quarters, Thiruvananthapuram

Contact Details: +91-471 272 1547, +91-471 272 2768

E-mail: hitechcell@keralapolice.gov.in

➢ Meghalaya

SCRB,Superintendent of Police, Meghalaya

Contact Details: +91 98630 64997

E-mail: scrb-meg@nic.in

➢ Orissa

CID, Crime Branch, Orissa

Ph: +91 94374 50370

E-mail: splcidcb.orpol@nic.in

➢ Bihar

Cyber Crime Investigation Unit

Dy.S.P.Kotwali Police Station, Patna

Ph: +91 94318 18398

E-mail: cciu-bih@nic.in

➤ Punjab

Cyber Crime Police Station, DSP Cyber Crime,

S.A.S Nagar,Patiala, Punjab

Ph: +91 172 2748 100

➤ Uttar Pradesh

Cyber Complaints Redressal Cell, Nodal Officer Cyber cell Agra, Agra Range 7,Kutchery Road, Baluganj,Agra-232001

Uttar Pradesh

Ph:919410837559

e-mail: info@cybercellagra.com

➢ West Bengal

CID, Cyber Crime, West Bengal

Ph: +9133 24506163

e-mail:occyber@cidwestbengal.gov.in

➢ UttaraKhand

Special Task Force Office

Sub Inspector of Police, Dehradoon

Ph: +91 135 2640982, +91 94123 70272

e-mail:dgc-police-us@nic.in

THANK YOU

I would like to thank you all for reading this book and I hope that you have been understood the reality of Internet. All the teenagers who read this book should be remember always these all facts, tips which I had given into this book because it is very useful and important to know for every teenager who is using Internet. I only want to say you that do not explore your real life on Internet because there is a big difference in your real life and Internet life. Both are totally different from each other where the reality is also be different. So, always think before to do any activity on Internet. Is it right or wrong for you??

Internet is not for the fun which you do on it. It is a way to get any help which you want. Now the choice is yours that how you use it? For your help or your fun. This is a very important topic for all of teenagers who use the Internet and spend their whole day on it because if it can give you fun then also can destroy your life. Your one mistake can become a very dangerous for you which you do on Internet. So never use it a lot or make fun. Its your duty to inform others about the Internet and give the advice to them "how they should be use the Internet? ".

SAGAR CHANDOLA

CPSIA information can be obtained at www.ICGtesting.com
Printed in the USA
LVOW07s1937151015

458419LV00027B/577/P

9 781505 933451